I0468215

One Family, Two Worlds:

A Story about Total Estate Planning

Look beyond the need and ask "Why?"

Jennifer R. Lewis Kannegieter

© 2016 by Jennifer R. Lewis Kannegieter

All Rights Reserved.

No part of this book may be reproduced, stored in a retrieval system, or transmitted in any form or by any means without the prior written permission of Jennifer R. Lewis Kannegieter.

ISBN-13: 978-1530543014

ISBN-10: 1530543010

This book is intended for informational purposes only.
No part of this book shall be construed as legal advice.
No attorney-client relationship is formed by use of this book.

Table of Contents

Introduction:
Do You Understand the Difference
a Will Could Make For Your Family?

If you are like most Americans then you know that you need a Will, but actually completing a Will is a task you have not yet accomplished. You probably have a million different excuses for not having a Will yet.

- *I don't have anything worth making a Will for.*

- *I will get it done when I have the money for it.*

- *Our family is not yet complete, we'll get a Will done when it is.*

- *My family knows what I want.*

- *There is nothing to fight over.*

Believe me, as an estate planning attorney I have heard them all. It is easy to give an excuse when the reasons why you "need" a Will center on the abstract "it is the adult thing to do." I can talk all day about the nuts and bolts of estate planning: what a Will is; why you might need a trust; and how the probate process works. But the truth of the matter is, none of that adequately explains why you need to complete your estate planning, which quite simply is this:

Completing a Will and other estate planning documents can make a world of difference for your loved ones.

To understand just how important *Total Estate Planning* is for your family's protection and your own peace of mind, read Alex and Christina's story from two different alternate realities. In one world tragedy strikes before Alex and Christina have taken any steps to get their affairs in order. In the other world, Alex and Christina have completed a *Total Estate Plan*. While Alex and Christina are fictional, this story is based on real life cases.

One Family, Two Worlds: Meet Alex and Christina

Alex and Christina are your typical "All American" couple. College sweethearts they have been married for ten years. Alex is an engineer; Christina is a high school teacher. They have two beautiful children — six year old Christopher and two year old Lexi.

On a quiet May evening Alex and Christina have plans for a night out in celebration of their 10th anniversary. With two young children and busy careers, they don't get out enough. Before leaving the children with Tina, their trusted babysitter, they kiss the kids goodnight and make sure Tina knows their plans for the evening.

Alex and Christina have a lovely dinner together. They are on their way home when a truck swerves into their lane, hitting their Honda Civic head on. Christina dies instantly. Alex is severely injured and unable to communicate. He is airlifted to the hospital and rushed into surgery.

Without an Estate Plan...

While they know they should have a Will, they just have not gotten around to doing one yet. They are always so busy. They are not sure where to start or who to talk to. There is always something else to spend the money on. They are young and healthy. They might have more kids. They will get it done before they need it. Besides, their families know what they would want. To read about what happens to Alex and Christina's family in a world without an estate plan, turn to page 11.

With a Total Estate Plan...

Christina is a planner and a bit of a worrier. When she first got pregnant with Christopher she insisted they have their Wills done. She found a lawyer to assist with their *Total Estate Planning*. Christina wanted to make sure that if anything were to happen, her kids would be taken care of and her family would know what to do. As part of their estate plan, Alex, Christina, and their lawyer prepared all sorts of documents and instructions for loved ones. Two weeks after Lexi was born, Christina and Alex met again with the attorney to update their documents. To read about what happens to Alex and Christina's family in a world with a *Total Estate Plan*, turn to page 27.

Alex and Christina: Without an Estate Plan

It has gotten late and Tina is wondering where Alex and Christina are. They are never late. She calls their cell phones only to get voicemail. She calls the restaurant and learns they left hours ago. She is freaking out and not sure what to do or who to call. Hours after the accident, the police show up at the door. They have come to break the news to Alex and Christina's family.

Temporary Care of the Children

Tina is devastated by the news. The cops learn about Christopher and Lexi and know they need to make sure the children are taken care of. Tina is just a babysitter and has no legal authority over the children. Tina has heard Alex and Christina mention their

11

families, but she doesn't have names or phone numbers for any of their relatives. The police contact CPS who arrange for Christopher and Lexi to be placed in emergency temporary foster care.

A sleeping Christopher is woken up by an emotional Tina and a social worker he has never seen before. He has no idea what is going on. His parents are missing, his babysitter keeps crying, and there are police officers at his house. No one can really answer his questions. Tina has packed an overnight bag and makes sure that each child has his or her lovey. The social worker takes the kids to a foster home. By the following morning Alex and Christina's parents and siblings have all been notified of the crash. Alex has survived surgery but is now in a coma. It is unknown whether he will survive.

Medical Decisions

Meanwhile, Alex remains in the hospital and the doctors need guidance from his family on how to treat him. Since his wife is dead, they look to his parents.

Alex's parents have been divorced for 25 years and the last thing they ever agreed on was to get a divorce. They have different opinions on how Alex should be treated, where he should be cared for, and who should be treating him. A guardianship court proceeding is needed to determine who will be making these decisions for Alex. His parents spend thousands of dollars (and several precious hours) on the court proceeding. Eventually Alex's mom is appointed guardian and granted the power to make decisions about Alex's care.

After months of holding onto hope Alex will get better, he takes a turn for the worse. With the help of his doctors, Alex's mom reaches the decision to remove him from life support. While part of her knows this was the right decision, it is something that haunts her for the rest of her life.

Alex's mom plans an elaborate funeral – in part to cope with her own grief and to "compensate" for the decision to remove life support. The funeral is much more than anything Alex would have chosen on his own and it is paid out of his estate.

Financial Control

While Alex was hospitalized a conservatorship needed to be established in court so that Alex's money can be accessed to pay the family's mortgage and other bills in the hopes of keeping things running for when Alex woke up. Much like the process of appointing a guardian for Alex, his parents once again go to court so that a conservator can be granted the power to control Alex's finances.

Administration of the Estate

With both Alex and Christina gone, the families must move forward with administering the estate and determining who will raise Christopher and Lexi. Alex's brother, Adam, offers to serve as personal representative (executor) of the estate. Adam is the most serious, organized, everything by-the-rules, "numbers" guy you've ever met – so nobody in either family objects to this. Always the practical guy, Adam does not understand why anyone might keep something for sentimental reasons. Upon being appointed by the court, Adam gets right to work on his duties. Alex and Christina's records are a mess and the administration is a long and expensive process.

As part of the estate administration, Adam needs to deal with all of the personal property Alex and Christina have accumulated through the years. Adam feels the best course of action is to sell everything at an estate sale so there is more cash to set aside for Christopher and Lexi – so that is what he does.

Adam sells the painting Alex and Christina purchased on their honeymoon. He sells all of Christina's jewelry, including her wedding ring, the gifts Alex purchased for her, the pearls given to her by Alex's grandmother, and the jewelry passed down to her by her own grandmother. He sells Alex's wedding ring and the tie tack Christina just recently had made with both of their kids birthstones. He sells the solid oak bedroom set hand carved by Christina's great-great-grandfather. He even sells the footlockers full of mementos from the lives of Alex and Christina.

Permanent Guardians

Meanwhile, the families are caught up in a court battle over who will raise Christopher and Lexi. There are three options: Andrea and Chad; Joan and Tom; and Erica.

- **Andrea and Chad.** Andrea and Chad are a married couple in their mid-thirties. They have been married for ten years and have three children ages 5, 8, and 11. Andrea is an at-home mom, while Chad works full-time. They own a four bedroom home in the country.

- **Joan and Tom.** Joan and Tom are a married couple in their late forties. They have been happily married for thirty years. Their two children are grown and out of the house. Joan works part-time and Tom has a lot of paid time off available to him. They own a beautiful three bedroom house in an affluent suburb.

- **Erica.** Erica is 24. She is single, but recently started dating someone. She is currently in grad-school and has never worked full-time. She rents a two bedroom apartment in the city.

All parties insist Alex and Christina would have wanted the children raised by themselves, and are confident that they can provide the best home for Christopher and Lexi. The decision of who will raise Alex and Christina's children is left up to a judge who has never met Alex, Christina, Christopher, or Lexi. The Judge must make this decision based only upon the information provided in the court file.

If you were the judge, who would you choose? Andrea and Chad? Joan and Tom? Erica? Take a look to see what life was like with your chosen guardian, then go read 'A Parent's Legacy' without an estate plan on page 25.

- **To choose Andrea and Chad turn to page 18.**
- **To choose Joan and Tom turn to page 21.**
- **To choose Erica turn to page 23.**

The Judge Chooses Andrea and Chad...

Andrea is Alex's sister. She is also the last person Alex and Christina would have chosen to raise their children. Andrea and Chad's values and life style are vastly different than Alex and Christina's.

As parents, they can be rather uninvolved with their children. Neither one thinks education is important. As long as the schools are not calling them to complain about their children's behavior, attendance, or grades, they are happy. They don't understand why you would pay for your child to be involved in dance or soccer or anything else. Their children spend their free time running free outside or watching television and playing video games.

Andrea and Chad spend a lot of time with Chad's brothers, but very little time with Andrea's family. Alex was her favorite brother. Her other brother Adam has always been too uptight in her opinion. Her mother is overbearing, and while she gets along with her father, he's never been very good at maintaining relationships.

Visits with Andrea's family are few and far between.

As guardians for Christopher and Lexi, Andrea and Chad are happy to welcome them into their home. Christopher and Lexi quickly find themselves surrounded by the chaos caused by their cousins. They have fun with all of the commotion, but also struggle to adjust to a world without rules and structure.

Over the first couple of years, Christopher and Lexi are able to see their grandparents and other aunts and uncles. But Andrea finds it to be a burden to arrange visits with Christina's family, and Chad has never really liked them, so the visits soon stop. When Andrea's mother expresses concern over all of her grandchildren, Andrea cuts her out of their lives too. Christopher and Lexi have no contact with any other relatives outside of Andrea, Chad, and their children.

Andrea and Chad raise Christopher and Lexi just like their own children. All though they are both bright, they were never encouraged to do their school work and received below-average grades. They never participated in sports or activities. By middle school they were experimenting with sex, alcohol, and drugs, and had gotten in trouble for shoplifting and vandalism. By the time they have graduated high school; neither child has much ambition in life.

The Judge Chooses Joan and Tom...

Joan is Christina's older cousin. They were very close growing up, although they have drifted apart over the years. While Alex and Christina would have acknowledged Joan and Tom are loving parents who did a good job raising their own children – they would not have been Alex and Christina's top choice.

Although she has a heart of gold, Joan has a strong personality that can be hard to take. She can be domineering and things are either her way or no way. Tom can be distant and a workaholic. As parents they had very high standards for their children and constantly pushed them a little too hard to exceed. Joan is a bit of a "helicopter" parent.

Joan is excited at the prospect of being a parent again. Parenting was the one thing she enjoyed the most in her life. She jumps right in – setting up bedrooms for Christopher and Lexi and enrolling them in school, soccer, dance, and piano. On the weekends she plans family trips to museums. Christopher and Lexi are so busy they don't even have a chance to think about all the changes that have occurred.

Joan loves to entertain and is big on family relationships. She hosts most extended family holidays and plans an annual family reunion for her side of the family. Because she values family, she acknowledges that Alex's family should be a part of the children's lives and encourages their relationship with the kids. It is a very nice sentiment, although the court battle caused a lot of hard feelings on both sides of the family and Joan's overbearing personality can be hard for others to take.

Joan and Tom push the children not only to succeed, but to exceed all expectations. They are valedictorians and team captains. They are each awarded generous scholarships to prestigious schools.

By all appearances the children are successful. But through the years Joan and Tom's over-the-top behavior placed a lot of stress on the children. Christopher suffers from anxiety and Lexi has self-esteem issues and an undiagnosed eating disorder.

The Judge Chooses Erica...

Erica is Christina's younger sister. She is the person Alex and Christina would have chosen to raise Lexi and Christopher if they had prepared an estate plan. They share the same values and general approach to life. Although she is young and often thought to be irresponsible, Alex and Christina believed she would be the one person who could raise their children the way they would have wanted to.

Erica takes the children in with open arms and Christopher and Lexi are very comfortable with Auntie Erica. Erica works hard to maintain the children's relationships with her extended family, Alex's family, and their former neighbors and classmates. She tries to parent Christopher and Lexi how she believes Alex and Christina would have. Erica struggles with the day to day challenges of parenting. She is constantly second guessing herself and asking how Alex and Christina would have responded in any given situation. Erica believes the judge's decision to appoint her as guardian of the children is often criticized by many of her extended family members. The custody battle caused an irreparable rift in her relationship with Cousin Joan. Erica feels pressure to be "the perfect parent" and is reluctant to seek any help from family. While Erica encourages the children's relationships with extended family, her own relationships are strained. The children pick up on this and feel like the tension is their fault.

A Parent's Legacy

Prior to closing the probate of the estate, a conservatorship is established to manage all of the money from the estate for the benefit of Christopher and Lexi. Each child is to receive half of the proceeds. Money is available to them, subject to approval, for their care and well-being during their childhood.

After Christopher's 18th birthday he receives a check for the remaining funds from his share. He purchases a classic Ford Mustang and a Harley. Feeling rich, and perhaps rebellious, he goes on spending sprees and takes lavish vacations. The money has run out by the time he is 23.

Lexi is determined to manage her inheritance better than her brother did and makes more modest purchases when she receives her money. But she starts "loaning" money to her worthless boyfriend and his friends and by the time she is 25 all she is left with is a broken heart and loans that will never be paid back.

Christopher remembers his parents, but as each

year passes the memories become foggier and foggier. He knows he used to love listening to his dad laugh, but he no longer remembers what that sounded like. He remembers his mom used to sing all the time, but he has forgotten the sound of her voice and the words of her songs. Lexi was so young when her parents died, she really doesn't know them at all. She has a few pictures that managed to survive the estate administration and she has heard a few stories over the years, but for all practical purposes they are strangers.

Alex and Christina:
With a Total Estate Plan

It has gotten late and Tina is wondering where Alex and Christina are. They are never late. She calls their cell phones only to get voicemail. She calls the restaurant and learns they left hours ago. She gets out the household binder Christina keeps and finds the information Christina had told her would be there. She calls Christina's cousin Joan, the first contact on the emergency contact list. Joan comes right over and together Joan and Tina call the police. While they are on the phone, the cops arrive at the house to break the news about Alex and Christina's accident.

A Temporary Guardian

Joan takes control of the situation. She provides

the cops information on Alex and Christina's next-of-kin. Joan provides the officers with the temporary custodian designation Alex and Christina prepared with their lawyer granting her authority to care for the children. The cops leave the house to continue with their investigation. Joan, with Tina's help, contacts family members. Finally, Tina heads home, and Joan tries to catch some sleep on the couch.

Christopher and Lexi have slept through the entire commotion. When they awake in the morning, Cousin Joan, a woman they have known their entire lives, and who has routinely cared for them, is there to greet them. Joan, as the legally designated temporary custodian, makes arrangements to care for Christopher and Lexi for the time-being.

A Health Care Directive

Meanwhile, Alex has survived surgery but has suffered significant brain damage and is now in a vegetative state. Alex has a Health Care Directive in which he appointed his brother Adam as his Health

Care Agent and provided instructions for the type of health care he wishes to receive. To Alex, quality of life is paramount. He does not want to be left to survive on machines. With the help of Alex's doctors, Adam is able to make decisions guided by Alex's clear wishes. Alex passes away peacefully, without spending months on life support. Alex's family plans his modest funeral, as requested by Alex.

Administration of the Estate

Alex and Christina appointed Alex's brother Adam as their personal administrator, the trustee in their wills, and the person to handle their estate. Understanding Adam's personality they also left him with instructions on how they wanted things taken care. Although Adam does not understand why Alex and Christina have accumulated so much "stuff" over the years, he is committed to doing what they have requested. All of their sentimental personal property is distributed according to their wishes, or held for safekeeping to be given to Christopher and Lexi when they are older. Because of the detailed instructions and records left by Christina and Alex, the estate administration is a quick and inexpensive process. A trust is set up, as established in their wills, for the benefit of Christopher and Lexi. The trust also provides a housing stipend for the children's guardian so that the children will be raised in the same school district they have always lived.

A Permanent Guardian

Alex and Christina chose Erica, Christina's sister, to raise Christopher and Lexi. While Erica is young and some people feel she is irresponsible, Erica loves her niece and nephew and shares the same values, and general approach to life as Alex and Christina. They know she will do a great job raising the children how they would want them raised.

After the funerals, Joan works with Erica to provide a smooth transition for the children. Even though Joan can't understand why Alex and Christina would have trusted their children with Erica, Joan is happy to help out any way she can since this is what

Alex and Christina would have wanted.

Erica finds parenting a bit overwhelming at first, but she has a supportive network of extended family on both sides. As part of her *Total Estate Plan*, Christina left her sister various letters with instructions and insight on how to parent the children. Erica finds great comfort in these letters over the years.

A Trust for the Children

Alex and Christina established a trust for the benefit of the children in their wills. Money is available to care for the children and to pay for their college education. Each child receives partial distributions (to spend however they like) at 25 and 30, and the remaining money at 35.

Although each child spent a little more than they should have at 25, by the time they were 30 they had a better understanding of the value of money. They were able to use the money to offset wedding costs, put towards a down payment of a house, and save for the future. When he received his final distribution,

Christopher started a college fund for each of his two kids.

Legacy Planning

Although Alex had called her crazy for doing it, Christina had insisted on legacy planning for their children. Alex and Christina had worked with their lawyer and had completed some legacy projects on their own.

After their parents' deaths, each child received a Legacy Book – a story about their parents and their family. These quickly became their favorite bedtime story. CDs Christina had recorded of her singing the children's favorite lullabies brought comfort to Christopher and Lexi long past the time when lullabies were "cool."

Alex and Christina had also created a Legacy Talk, an audio cd, to share all of the values they wanted their children to remember. This was something Erica and Adam waited until the children were 13 to share with the children.

On their own, Alex and Christina had prepared various letters to be given at different points of their children's lives – various birthdays or milestones. When Lexi graduates college she is presented with her great-grandmother's pearls and a letter from her parents explaining how these pearls were a graduation gift to her great-grandmother in honor of becoming the first woman in the family with a college degree. When Christopher is given his father's tie tack after the birth of his first child, he also given a letter from his parents about the joys, and concerns, a new baby brings.

Although their parents have been gone a long time, Christopher and Lexi always felt like Mom and Dad were there for them. While the memories of their parents when they were alive have faded, new memories were created due to the books, CDs, letters, and gifts that were part of Alex and Christina's legacy planning.

So Now What?

Now that you have seen what a profound and lasting impact a *Total Estate Plan* can have on a family it is time to get serious. Completing an estate plan is not a daunting task to be feared. In fact, the hardest part is making the commitment to get it done. The *Total Estate Planning* process is designed to be as easy as possible, with five simple steps:

1. Make the decision to do it. Contact me at **jennifer@lewisklaw.com** or **(763) 244-2949** to request an introductory packet and schedule your *Personal Strategy Session*.

2. Complete the *Personal Inventory and Assessment* - a client questionnaire that asks for the information needed to prepare your estate

planning documents. Do not worry if you cannot answer all of the questions.

3. Attend the *Personal Strategy Session*. You'll receive an individualized education on the nuts and bolts of estate planning and we will identify the best way to protect your family and fulfill your wishes. At the end of the session you'll select the *Total Estate Planning* package that is right for you and retain my services.

4. Relax. I will take care of drafting your *Total Estate Plan*. The hard work for you is over.

5. Come back for the final signing meeting. We'll review and sign the documents. I will prepare your estate plan binder and instructions. Your *Total Estate Plan* is complete.

Just five simple steps for your peace of mind and your family's protection. Every week I am confronted with another situation made worse by an individual's failure to proactively plan ahead. Do not let that happen to your family. If you are ready to get started contact me today.

About The Author

Jennifer R. Lewis Kannegieter, is a mother, author, Minnesota estate planning and family law attorney, founding lawyer at Lewis Kannegieter Law, Ltd., and *Your Minnesota Family Lawyer.*

With an approach based on common sense and education, Jennifer provides stability and security for families through a variety of estate planning and family law services.

Jennifer R. Lewis Kannegieter

Jennifer takes a holistic approach to her law practice. She guides her clients through the legal process, taking the time to explain possible options and outcomes; helping each client reach the best decisions for themselves and their families. She recognizes that every client has different needs and circumstances. Because Jennifer understands that the legal issue is just one aspect of the entire situation she takes a *Total Approach*, considering the personal, emotional, physical, and financial needs of her clients in addition to the legal needs.

Jennifer resides in Monticello, Minnesota with her family where she is an active member of the community. For more information visit her website at **www.JenniferLewisK.com**.

www.ingramcontent.com/pod-product-compliance
Lightning Source LLC
Chambersburg PA
CBHW070421190526
45169CB00003B/1362